PYTHON FROM SCRATCH

A Beginner's Journey to
Programming Excellence

Olanrewaju Sanni

ISBN: 9798859352678

Cover design by: Art Painter
Library of Congress Control Number: 2018675309
Printed in the United States of America

I dedicate this book to my Lord Jesus Christ, the Saviour of my soul.

CONTENTS

Title Page

Copyright

Dedication

Preface

Introduction to Python   1

Basic Syntax and Data Types   4

Control Structures   8

Functions and Modules   12

File Handling   16

Object-Oriented Programming (OOP) in Python   20

Advanced Topics in Python   24

Debugging and Testing   29

Debugging and Testing   33

Application Development   37

Best Practices and Conclusion   41

Appendix   45

Conclusion   50

PREFACE

Welcome to the exciting world of Python programming! Whether you are a beginner or an experienced programmer, this textbook aims to equip you with the knowledge and skills necessary to become proficient in Python.

Python, known for its simplicity and versatility, has gained immense popularity among developers worldwide. Its readable syntax and extensive library support make it an ideal choice for a wide range of applications, from web development and data analysis to artificial intelligence and automation.

This textbook serves as a comprehensive guide to learning Python from scratch. It is designed to cater to different learning styles and provides a structured approach to understanding the language and its various concepts.

Key Features Of This Textbook:

- Theory and Practical Examples: Each chapter introduces fundamental concepts, followed by practical examples that demonstrate the application of those concepts in real-world scenarios. This combination of theory and hands-on experience ensures a well-rounded understanding of Python programming.

- Projects and Exercises: Throughout the book, you will find numerous projects and exercises that encourage you to apply your knowledge and test your skills. These activities are designed to reinforce your learning and enhance problem-solving abilities.

- Clear Explanations: We believe in simplicity and clarity, and our explanations reflect that belief. Complex concepts are broken down into easily understandable explanations, enabling you to grasp even the most challenging topics with ease.

- Best Practices and Tips: In addition to teaching you the syntax and core concepts of Python, we provide best practices and tips to help you write clean, efficient, and maintainable code. These insights will enhance your programming skills and make your code more professional.

Who Is This Textbook For?

This textbook is suitable for:

- Beginners: If you have no prior programming experience or are new to Python, this book will guide you through the fundamentals and gradually build your skills.

- Students: Whether studying computer science or a related field, this textbook can serve as a companion for learning Python in an academic setting.

- Self-Learners: If you prefer self-paced learning, this book provides a structured curriculum that allows you to learn at your own pace and track your progress.

How To Use This Textbook:

To make the most of this textbook, we recommend following these guidelines:

1. Read each chapter carefully, ensuring you understand the concepts presented before moving on to the next chapter.

2. Complete the exercises and projects at the end of each chapter to reinforce your understanding and solidify your skills.

3. Take advantage of the additional resources available online, such as code samples, supplementary materials, and interactive quizzes, which can further enhance your learning experience.

4. Practice regularly by working on personal coding projects or solving coding challenges on platforms like HackerRank or LeetCode. This will help you apply what you've learned and gain confidence in your abilities.

We believe that anyone can learn to code, and our goal is to provide you with a strong foundation in Python programming. As you embark on this journey, remember to stay curious, be persistent, and never hesitate to seek help when needed. With dedication and practice, you will soon find yourself confidently writing Python code and developing exciting applications.

We would like to extend our gratitude to all the contributors, reviewers, and editors who have helped shape this textbook. Their expertise and commitment have been invaluable in creating a resource that we hope will inspire and empower you on your Python programming journey.

So, let's dive into the world of Python and embark on an incredible adventure of coding possibilities. Happy learning!

Olanrewaju Sanni

INTRODUCTION TO PYTHON

A. What Is Python?

Python is a high-level, interpreted programming language known for its simplicity and readability. It was created by Guido van Rossum and first released in 1991. Python emphasizes code readability with its clean and intuitive syntax, making it an ideal language for beginners and experienced programmers alike.

B. Advantages Of Python

Python offers several advantages that make it a popular choice among developers:

1. Easy to Learn and Use: Python's simple syntax and straightforward structure make it easy to grasp for beginners. The language focuses on code readability, allowing developers to write clean and concise code.

2. Versatility: Python is a versatile language that can be used for various purposes such as web development, data analysis, scientific computing, artificial intelligence, automation, and more. It has an extensive standard library and a rich ecosystem of third-party libraries, making it suitable for a wide range of applications.

3. Cross-platform Compatibility: Python is a platform-independent language. It can run on different operating systems like Windows, macOS, and Linux without any modifications, making it highly portable.

4. Large and Active Community: Python has a large and active community of developers who contribute to its growth and provide support to fellow programmers. The community-driven nature ensures the availability of resources, libraries, and frameworks to facilitate development.

5. Integration Capabilities: Python can easily integrate with other languages such as C, C++, and Java, allowing developers to leverage existing code or utilize specific features from other languages.

C. Setting Up Python Development Environment

To start programming in Python, you need to set up a development environment. Here are the steps to get started:

1. Install Python: Visit the official Python website (python.org) and download the appropriate installer for your operating system. Follow the installation instructions, and make sure to add Python to your system's PATH variable.

2. Verify Installation: Open a terminal or command prompt and type "python --version" to check if Python is properly installed and displaying the version number.

3. Text Editor or Integrated Development Environment (IDE): Choose a text editor or an IDE that suits your preferences and requirements. Some popular options include Visual Studio Code,

PyCharm, Atom, Sublime Text, and IDLE (which comes bundled with Python).

4. Run Your First Python Program: Create a new file with a .py extension in your text editor or IDE. Write a simple "Hello, World!" program:

```python
print("Hello, World!")
```

Save the file and execute it by running the Python interpreter on the command line, specifying the file's path:

```
python path/to/your/file.py
```

You should see the output "Hello, World!" displayed in the console.

Congratulations! You have successfully set up your Python development environment and are ready to start coding in Python.

BASIC SYNTAX AND DATA TYPES

A. Variables And Assignments

In Python, variables are used to store values. You can assign a value to a variable using the assignment operator (=). Variables can store different types of data such as numbers, strings, lists, etc.

Example:

```python
name = "John"
age = 25
```

B. Numeric Data Types (Int, Float)

Python provides two main numeric data types: integers (int) and floating-point numbers (float). Integers represent whole numbers, while floating-point numbers represent decimal numbers.

Example:

```python
```

```python
x = 10      # integer
y = 4.5     # float
```

C. Strings And String Operations

Strings are sequences of characters enclosed in single or double quotation marks. Python provides various string operations, including concatenation, slicing, and formatting.

Example:
```python
message = "Hello, World!"
print(message)

# String concatenation
name = "John"
greeting = "Hello, " + name + "!"
print(greeting)

# String slicing
text = "Python is awesome"
print(text[0:6]) # Output: Python

# String formatting
quantity = 3
item = "books"
print("I have {} {}.".format(quantity, item))  # Output: I have 3
```

books.

` ` `

D. Lists And Tuples

Lists and tuples are used to store multiple items in a single variable. Lists are mutable, meaning their elements can be modified, added, or removed. Tuples, on the other hand, are immutable and cannot be changed once created.

Example:

` ` `python

```
# Lists
fruits = ["apple", "banana", "orange"]
print(fruits[1])   # Output: banana

fruits.append("grape")
print(fruits)     # Output: ['apple', 'banana', 'orange', 'grape']

# Tuples
student = ("John", 25, "Mathematics")
print(student[0])  # Output: John
```

` ` `

E. Dictionaries And Sets

Dictionaries are unordered collections of key-value pairs. Each value is associated with a unique key, allowing quick access to values based on their keys. Sets, on the other hand, are unordered collections of unique elements.

Example:

```python
# Dictionaries
person = {"name": "John", "age": 25, "city": "New York"}
print(person["age"])   # Output: 25

person["job"] = "Engineer"
print(person)          # Output: {'name': 'John', 'age': 25, 'city': 'New York', 'job': 'Engineer'}

# Sets
fruits = {"apple", "banana", "orange"}
fruits.add("grape")
print(fruits)
# Output: {'banana', 'grape', 'apple', 'orange'}
```

Understanding the basic syntax and data types in Python is essential as they form the building blocks for writing programs in the language. With this foundation, you can begin exploring more complex concepts and features offered by Python.

CONTROL STRUCTURES

In Python programming, control structures are essential for directing the flow of your code and handling different scenarios. Let's explore four important control structures in Python:

A. Conditional Statements (If, Elif, Else):

Conditional statements allow you to execute specific blocks of code based on certain conditions. The "if" statement is the most basic conditional statement, which checks a condition and executes a block of code if it evaluates to true. You can also include "elif" (short for else if) to check additional conditions, and "else" to provide a default block of code if none of the conditions are met.

For example:
```python
num = 7

if num < 0:
    print("Negative number")
elif num == 0:
    print("Zero")
```

```
else:
    print("Positive number")
```
```

## B. Looping Structures (For, While):

Looping structures allow you to repeat a block of code multiple times. The "for" loop is used to iterate over a sequence (such as a list, string, or range of numbers), executing the block of code for each item in the sequence. On the other hand, the "while" loop repeats the block of code as long as a specified condition remains true.

For example:
```python
# Using a for loop
fruits = ["apple", "banana", "cherry"]
for fruit in fruits:
    print(fruit)

# Using a while loop
count = 0
while count < 5:
    print(count)
    count += 1
```
```

C. Break And Continue Statements:

The "break" statement allows you to prematurely exit a loop when a certain condition is met. It is useful when you want to terminate the loop before it reaches its natural end. The "continue" statement, on the other hand, jumps to the next iteration of the loop, bypassing the remaining code in the current iteration.

For example:

```python
# Using break statement
fruits = ["apple", "banana", "cherry"]
for fruit in fruits:
    if fruit == "banana":
        break
    print(fruit)

# Using continue statement
for i in range(10):
    if i % 2 == 0:
        continue
    print(i)
```

D. Exception Handling:

Exception handling is crucial for handling errors and preventing your program from crashing. By using the "try" and "except" statements, you can catch and handle exceptions that may occur during the execution of your code. This allows you to gracefully handle errors and continue with the program's execution, preventing it from abruptly terminating.

For example:

```python
try:
    x = 5 / 0
except ZeroDivisionError:
    print("Cannot divide by zero")
```

By understanding and utilizing these control structures effectively, you can create more robust and flexible Python programs. They provide you with the ability to make decisions, repeat tasks, handle errors, and ultimately control the behavior of your program.

FUNCTIONS AND MODULES

In Python programming, functions and modules play a crucial role in organizing and reusing code. Let's explore four important concepts related to functions and modules:

A. Defining And Calling Functions:

Functions are blocks of reusable code that perform a specific task. They allow you to break down your program into smaller, manageable pieces. To define a function, you use the "def" keyword followed by the function name and parentheses. You can also include parameters within the parentheses if the function requires input. To call or invoke a function, you simply use its name followed by parentheses.

For example:

```python
def greet():
    print("Hello, how are you?")

greet()  # calling the greet() function
```

B. Function Arguments And Return Values:

Functions can accept arguments, which allow you to pass data into the function for processing. You can define parameters within the parentheses when defining the function and then use those parameters inside the function's block. Additionally, functions can return values using the "return" statement, which allows you to obtain results or pass data back to the caller.

For example:

```python
def multiply(x, y):
    return x * y


result = multiply(5, 3)
print(result)
```

C. Understanding Scope And Local Vs. Global Variables:

Scope refers to the region of a program where a variable is accessible. In Python, variables defined inside a function are considered local variables and can only be accessed within that function. On the other hand, variables defined outside any function are considered global variables and can be accessed anywhere in the program. It is important to understand scope to prevent naming conflicts and properly manage variables.

For example:

```python
def multiply(x, y):
    z = x * y  # local variable
    return z

result = multiply(5, 3)
print(result)

x = 10  # global variable

def update_global_var():
    global x  # accessing the global variable
    x = 20

update_global_var()
print(x)
```

D. Using Modules And Importing Libraries:

Python provides a wide range of modules and libraries that extend its functionality. A module is a file containing Python definitions and statements that can be imported and used in other programs. Importing a module allows you to access its functions, classes, and variables. You can import a module using the "import" keyword, and then use its contents using the module name followed by a dot operator.

For example:

```python
# Importing the math module
import math

# Using functions from the math module
x = math.sqrt(25)
print(x)

# Importing specific functions from a module
from random import randint

# Using the imported function
y = randint(1, 100)
print(y)
```

By understanding and leveraging the power of functions and modules, you can create modular, reusable, and well-organized code in Python. Functions help you break down complex tasks into simpler ones, while modules bring in additional functionality from external sources.

FILE HANDLING

File handling is an essential part of any programming language, including Python. It allows you to read, write, and manage different types of files. Let's explore three important concepts related to file handling:

A. Reading And Writing Files:

Python provides built-in functions for reading and writing files. To read a file, you can use the `open()` function, which opens a file and returns a file object. You can then use various methods like `read()`, `readline()`, or `readlines()` to retrieve the contents of the file. Similarly, to write to a file, you can open it in a specific mode (such as "w" for write) and use the `write()` or `writelines()` method.

For example:
```python
# Reading a file
file = open("example.txt", "r")
content = file.read()
print(content)
file.close()

# Writing to a file
```

```
file = open("example.txt", "w")
file.write("This is some text.")
file.close()
```

B. Working With Text And Csv Files:

In addition to reading and writing plain text files, Python provides modules like `csv` for working with comma-separated value (CSV) files. The `csv` module allows you to easily read and write data from/to CSV files using its reader and writer objects. This module simplifies tasks like parsing and splitting data based on delimiters.

For example:
```python
import csv

# Reading a CSV file
with open("data.csv", "r") as file:
    reader = csv.reader(file)
    for row in reader:
        print(row)

# Writing to a CSV file
data = [["Name", "Age", "Country"],
        ["John", "25", "USA"],
        ["Jane", "30", "Canada"]]
```

```python
with open("output.csv", "w", newline=") as file:
    writer = csv.writer(file)
    writer.writerows(data)
```
` ` `

C. File Management (Opening, Closing, And Renaming):

When working with files, it's important to properly manage them by opening and closing them. The `open()` function returns a file object that should be closed after use to free up system resources. To close a file, you can use the `close()` method. Additionally, Python allows you to rename a file using the `os` module's `rename()` function.

For example:
` ` `python

```python
# Opening and closing a file
file = open("example.txt", "r")
# Do some operations on the file
file.close()

# Renaming a file
import os

os.rename("example.txt", "new_example.txt")
```
` ` `

Proper file management ensures that your program interacts with files efficiently and prevents any potential resource leaks. Whether you need to read and write regular text files or work with more complex file formats like CSV, Python provides flexible and convenient methods to handle various file-related tasks.

OBJECT-ORIENTED PROGRAMMING (OOP) IN PYTHON

Object-Oriented Programming (OOP) is a programming paradigm that organizes code into objects, which are instances of classes. Python supports OOP, and it offers various features and concepts to help you build modular and reusable code. Let's delve into some key concepts related to OOP in Python:

A. Introduction To Oop Concepts:

OOP revolves around four main concepts: encapsulation, inheritance, polymorphism, and abstraction. These concepts allow you to structure your code in a way that promotes code reusability, modularity, and flexibility.

B. Classes And Objects:

Classes are the blueprint or template for creating objects. They define attributes (variables) and methods (functions) that objects of that class can possess. To create an object, you instantiate a class by calling it as if it were a function. Objects are unique instances of a class, each with its own state and behavior.

For example:

```python
# Class definition
class Car:
    def __init__(self, brand, model):
        self.brand = brand
        self.model = model

    def drive(self):
        print(f"The {self.brand} {self.model} is driving.")

# Object instantiation
my_car = Car("Toyota", "Corolla")
my_car.drive()
```

C. Inheritance And Polymorphism:

Inheritance allows you to create new classes based on existing classes. The new class inherits the attributes and methods of the parent class, enabling code reuse. Polymorphism refers to the ability of objects of different classes to respond to the same method call based on their specific implementations.

For example:

```python
# Parent class
class Animal:
    def make_sound(self):
```

```
        pass

# Child classes inheriting from Animal
class Dog(Animal):
    def make_sound(self):
        print("Woof!")

class Cat(Animal):
    def make_sound(self):
        print("Meow!")

# Polymorphism in action
animals = [Dog(), Cat()]
for animal in animals:
    animal.make_sound()
```

D. Encapsulation And Abstraction:

Encapsulation is the process of bundling data (attributes) and methods together within a class and controlling access to them. It helps protect data integrity by providing methods that interact with the attributes. Abstraction focuses on exposing only essential information and hiding the internal implementation details.

For example:
```python
class BankAccount:
```

```python
    def __init__(self):
        self.balance = 0

    def deposit(self, amount):
        self.balance += amount

    def withdraw(self, amount):
        if self.balance >= amount:
            self.balance -= amount
        else:
            print("Insufficient funds.")

    def get_balance(self):
        return self.balance

# Encapsulation and abstraction in action
account = BankAccount()
account.deposit(100)
account.withdraw(50)
print(account.get_balance())
```

By incorporating OOP principles into your Python code, you can organize your codebase more effectively, improve code reusability, and create more maintainable and flexible applications.

ADVANCED TOPICS IN PYTHON

Python offers a wide range of advanced topics and modules that can enhance your programming skills and allow you to tackle more complex problems. Let's explore some of these topics:

A. Regular Expressions:

Regular expressions (regex) are a powerful tool for pattern matching and text manipulation. The `re` module in Python provides functions and methods for working with regular expressions. You can use regex to search, match, and manipulate strings based on specific patterns.

For example:

```python
import re

text = "Hello, my email address is john@example.com"
pattern = r"\b[A-Za-z0-9._%+-]+@[A-Za-z0-9.-]+\.[A-Z|a-z]{2,}\b"

matches = re.findall(pattern, text)
print(matches)
```

```
` ` `
```

B. Working With Dates And Time:

The `datetime` module in Python allows you to work with dates, times, and intervals. It provides classes and functions for creating, manipulating, and formatting dates and times. With this module, you can perform calculations, comparisons, and conversions involving dates and times.

For example:

```python
from datetime import datetime, timedelta

current_date = datetime.now()
print(current_date)

two_days_ago = current_date - timedelta(days=2)
print(two_days_ago)

formatted_date = current_date.strftime("%Y-%m-%d %H:%M:%S")
print(formatted_date)
```

C. Database Interaction (Sql And Sqlite):

Python provides various modules, such as `sqlite3` and `SQLAlchemy`, for interacting with databases. You can connect to databases, execute SQL queries, retrieve results, and perform transactions. SQLite is a built-in module in Python that allows you to work with lightweight, file-based databases.

For example (using `sqlite3`):

```python
import sqlite3

# Connect to a database
conn = sqlite3.connect('example.db')

# Create a cursor object
cursor = conn.cursor()

# Execute a query
cursor.execute("SELECT * FROM table_name")

# Fetch result
result = cursor.fetchall()
print(result)

# Close the connection
conn.close()
```

D. Web Scraping Using Beautiful Soup:

Beautiful Soup is a Python library for parsing HTML and XML documents. It provides easy-to-use methods to navigate and extract data from web pages. With Beautiful Soup, you can scrape web content, extract specific elements, and perform data extraction tasks.

For example:

```python
import requests
from bs4 import BeautifulSoup

url = "https://example.com"
response = requests.get(url)
soup = BeautifulSoup(response.text, "html.parser")

# Find specific elements
titles = soup.find_all("h1")
for title in titles:
    print(title.text)
```

E. Introduction To Gui Programming With Tkinter:

Tkinter is a standard Python library for creating Graphical User Interfaces (GUIs). It provides a set of widgets and tools for building windows, layouts, buttons, input fields, and more. Tkinter allows you to create interactive and user-friendly applications with ease.

For example:

```python
import tkinter as tk
```

```
window = tk.Tk()
window.title("My App")

label = tk.Label(window, text="Hello, World!")
label.pack()

button = tk.Button(window, text="Click Me!")
button.pack()

window.mainloop()
```
` ` `

By exploring these advanced topics in Python, you can expand your programming capabilities and build more sophisticated applications suited to your needs.

DEBUGGING AND TESTING

A. Identifying And Fixing Common Errors:

Debugging is an essential skill for any developer. Here are some common errors you may encounter while programming in Python and how to fix them:

1. Syntax errors: These occur when there is a mistake in the syntax of your code, such as missing colons or parentheses. The Python interpreter will raise a `SyntaxError` and provide a traceback indicating the location of the error.

2. Name errors: These occur when you reference a variable or function that has not been defined or is out of scope. Check if the variable or function name is spelled correctly and ensure it is defined before using it.

3. Type errors: These occur when there is a mismatch between the data types expected by an operation or function. For example, you might try to concatenate a string with an integer, which would raise a `TypeError`. Make sure the types are compatible or consider type conversions.

B. Using Debugging Tools (Print Statements,

Breakpoints):

Debugging tools can help you pinpoint and understand the cause of errors in your code. Some common debugging techniques include:

1. Print statements: Inserting print statements at various points in your code can help you understand the values of variables and the flow of execution. By printing the intermediate values, you can identify the problem area.

2. Logging: Instead of using print statements, you can use the logging module to log messages, warnings, and errors. This allows you to control the level of output and provides more flexibility in debugging different parts of your code.

3. Breakpoints: Integrated Development Environments (IDEs) like PyCharm and Visual Studio Code provide the ability to set breakpoints in your code. When the program reaches a breakpoint, it pauses execution, allowing you to inspect variables and step through the code line by line.

C. Unit Testing With Pytest:

Unit testing is a practice that involves testing individual parts (units) of your code to ensure they function correctly. PyTest is a popular Python testing framework that makes it easy to write and run tests.

To get started with PyTest, follow these steps:

1. Install PyTest by running `pip install pytest` in your command line.

2. Create a new Python file with test functions. Tests are written as functions starting with `test_` or methods starting with `test_`.

3. In each test function, use assertions to check if the output matches the expected result. If the assertion fails, PyTest will raise an assertion error.

4. To run the tests, navigate to the directory containing your test file in the command line and execute `pytest`.

Here's an example test using PyTest:

```python
# File: test_example.py

def add_numbers(a, b):
    return a + b

def test_add_numbers():
    assert add_numbers(2, 3) == 5
    assert add_numbers(10, 20) == 30
    assert add_numbers(-1, 1) == 0
```

When you run `pytest`, it will discover and run all the test functions/methods in your file, displaying the results.

By incorporating debugging techniques and writing tests with

PyTest, you can catch and fix errors in your code more efficiently, ensuring its reliability and quality.

DEBUGGING AND TESTING

A. Identifying And Fixing Common Errors:

Debugging is an essential skill for any developer. Here are some common errors you may encounter while programming in Python and how to fix them:

1. Syntax errors: These occur when there is a mistake in the syntax of your code, such as missing colons or parentheses. The Python interpreter will raise a `SyntaxError` and provide a traceback indicating the location of the error.

2. Name errors: These occur when you reference a variable or function that has not been defined or is out of scope. Check if the variable or function name is spelled correctly and ensure it is defined before using it.

3. Type errors: These occur when there is a mismatch between the data types expected by an operation or function. For example, you might try to concatenate a string with an integer, which would raise a `TypeError`. Make sure the types are compatible or consider type conversions.

B. Using Debugging Tools (Print Statements,

Breakpoints):

Debugging tools can help you pinpoint and understand the cause of errors in your code. Some common debugging techniques include:

1. Print statements: Inserting print statements at various points in your code can help you understand the values of variables and the flow of execution. By printing the intermediate values, you can identify the problem area.

2. Logging: Instead of using print statements, you can use the logging module to log messages, warnings, and errors. This allows you to control the level of output and provides more flexibility in debugging different parts of your code.

3. Breakpoints: Integrated Development Environments (IDEs) like PyCharm and Visual Studio Code provide the ability to set breakpoints in your code. When the program reaches a breakpoint, it pauses execution, allowing you to inspect variables and step through the code line by line.

C. Unit Testing With Pytest:

Unit testing is a practice that involves testing individual parts (units) of your code to ensure they function correctly. PyTest is a popular Python testing framework that makes it easy to write and run tests.

To get started with PyTest, follow these steps:

1. Install PyTest by running `pip install pytest` in your command line.

2. Create a new Python file with test functions. Tests are written as functions starting with `test_` or methods starting with `test_`.

3. In each test function, use assertions to check if the output matches the expected result. If the assertion fails, PyTest will raise an assertion error.

4. To run the tests, navigate to the directory containing your test file in the command line and execute `pytest`.

Here's an example test using PyTest:

```python
# File: test_example.py

def add_numbers(a, b):
    return a + b

def test_add_numbers():
    assert add_numbers(2, 3) == 5
    assert add_numbers(10, 20) == 30
    assert add_numbers(-1, 1) == 0
```

When you run `pytest`, it will discover and run all the test functions/methods in your file, displaying the results.

By incorporating debugging techniques and writing tests with

PyTest, you can catch and fix errors in your code more efficiently, ensuring its reliability and quality.

APPLICATION DEVELOPMENT

A. Building A Simple Console-Based Application:

Building a console-based application involves creating a program that interacts with the user through a command-line interface. Here are the basic steps to build a simple console-based application:

1. Design the application: Determine the purpose and functionality of your application. Define what inputs it needs from the user and what outputs it should produce.

2. Write the code: Implement the application's logic using a programming language like Python. Break down the functionality into smaller functions or modules to improve maintainability.

3. Use input/output functions: Utilize functions provided by your programming language to read input from the user and display output on the console. For example, in Python, you can use the `input()` function to read user input and the `print()` function to display output.

4. Test the application: Execute the application and test its behavior using different inputs to ensure it produces the expected

results. Make any necessary adjustments to fix any issues or errors.

B. Introduction To Web Development With Flask:

Web development with Flask is a popular framework for building web applications using Python. Flask provides a straightforward and flexible way to create web applications by leveraging the power of Python. Here's an overview of the steps involved in web development with Flask:

1. Install Flask: Start by installing Flask using the command `pip install flask`.

2. Setup a Flask application: Create a new Python file and import the Flask module. Define a Flask application object using `app = Flask(__name__)`.

3. Define routes and views: Define routes for different URLs and map them to view functions. View functions handle the logic for each route and return the response to the browser.

4. Create HTML templates: Use HTML templates to define the structure and layout of your web pages. Flask uses the Jinja templating engine, which allows you to include dynamic content in your templates.

5. Handle form submissions and user input: Implement forms in your templates to gather user input. Flask provides features to handle form submissions and process the data.

6. Test and debug: Run your Flask application and test it using

a web browser. Debug any issues or errors by examining error messages or using logging and debugging tools.

C. Gui Application Development With Tkinter:

Tkinter is a standard library in Python for creating GUI (Graphical User Interface) applications. It provides a set of widgets and tools to design and build user interfaces. Here are the basic steps to develop a GUI application with Tkinter:

1. Import the Tkinter module: Start by importing the Tkinter module using `import tkinter`. You can also use `import tkinter as tk` for easier access to Tkinter classes and functions.

2. Create a root window: Create the main window of your GUI application by creating an instance of the `tkinter.Tk` class.

3. Add widgets: Use various Tkinter widget classes (such as labels, buttons, entry fields, etc.) to add elements to your GUI application. Configure their properties and place them within the main window.

4. Define event handlers: Associate event handlers with user actions on your widgets. Event handlers respond to user interaction, such as button clicks or menu selections.

5. Run the main event loop: Use the `mainloop()` method on the root window to start the main event loop. This loop listens for events and updates the GUI accordingly.

6. Test and refine: Run your GUI application and test its functionality. Make adjustments to the layout, appearance, and

behavior based on user feedback or requirements.

By following these steps, you can develop both console-based and graphical applications using Python, opening up a wide range of possibilities for your projects.

BEST PRACTICES AND CONCLUSION

A. Writing Clean And Readable Code:

Writing clean and readable code is essential for maintaining code quality, collaboration, and future development. Here are some best practices to follow:

1. Use meaningful variable and function names: Choose descriptive names that accurately represent the purpose and functionality of your code.

2. Indentation and formatting: Ensure consistent indentation and proper formatting to improve code readability. Follow conventions such as using spaces or tabs consistently.

3. Avoid long lines and excessive nesting: Keep lines of code within a reasonable length and limit nested structures to enhance readability.

4. Break down complex logic: Divide complex tasks into smaller, manageable functions or methods. This improves code organization and makes it easier to understand and troubleshoot.

5. Remove unnecessary or redundant code: Regularly review your

codebase to eliminate unused variables, functions, or repetitive patterns. This simplifies code maintenance and reduces potential errors.

B. Commenting And Documentation:

Including comments and documentation in your code helps others understand its purpose and functionality. Follow these guidelines:

1. Use inline comments: Add comments within your code to explain the logic or provide context for specific sections. Ensure your comments are concise and relevant.

2. Document functions and modules: Write docstrings (comment blocks) for functions, classes, and modules. These docstrings describe their purpose, parameters, return values, and any exceptions they may raise.

3. Update documentation: Keep your documentation up-to-date as your code evolves. Update comments, docstrings, and any external documentation to reflect changes in functionality or behavior.

4. Utilize markup languages: Consider using markup languages (e.g., Markdown, reStructuredText) to create comprehensive documentation files separate from the code. These files can include explanations, examples, and usage instructions.

C. Version Control With Git:

Version control is crucial for managing code revisions, collaborating with others, and maintaining project history. Git is one of the most popular version control systems available. Follow these steps to get started:

1. Install Git: Download and install Git from the official website (htttps://git-scm.com/downloads) based on your operating system.

2. Initialize a Git repository: In your project's root directory, open a terminal and run `git init` to create a new Git repository for your project.

3. Commit changes: Use `git add <file>` to stage changes and `git commit -m "commit message"` to save those changes to the repository. Commit regularly to keep a reliable history of your code.

4. Branching and merging: Create branches to experiment with new features or bug fixes without affecting the main codebase. Merge branches back into the main branch (usually called `master`) once they're ready.

5. Collaborate and push changes: Set up a remote Git repository (e.g., GitHub, GitLab) to collaborate with others. Use `git push` to send your local commits to the remote repository and `git pull` to fetch updates made by others.

D. Resources For Further Learning And Development:

To continue learning and developing your skills, here are some helpful resources:

1. Online tutorials and courses: Explore online platforms like Udemy, Coursera, and Codecademy for various programming topics, including Python, web development, and more.

2. Documentation and official websites: Refer to official documentation for programming languages, frameworks, and tools you're interested in. They often provide detailed guides, tutorials, and examples.

3. Stack Overflow and developer communities: Visit Stack Overflow to find answers to specific coding questions or challenges. Participating in developer communities and forums can help you connect with experienced programmers and learn from their expertise.

4. Books and ebooks: Browse through programming books and ebooks that cover specific topics in-depth. Some popular Python books include "Python Crash Course" by Eric Matthes and "Fluent Python" by Luciano Ramalho.

Continuously improving your coding skills and staying up-to-date with industry trends and best practices will help you become a proficient and successful developer. Remember to practice regularly, seek feedback, and embrace the joy of learning new technologies and techniques. Good luck!

APPENDIX

In this appendix, you will find a collection of Python code examples that complement the main content of the textbook. These code snippets serve as practical demonstrations and reinforce the concepts discussed throughout the book. You can use them to practice programming, experiment with different techniques, and deepen your understanding of Python.

Note: It is recommended that readers have a basic understanding of Python programming before attempting to work with the code examples in this appendix. If you are new to Python, it is advisable to refer to the main content of the textbook first and then explore these code examples.

1. Hello World:

```python
print("Hello, World!")
```

2. Variables and Data Types:

```python
# Assigning values to variables
name = "John"
age = 25
```

```python
pi = 3.14
is_student = True

# Printing variable values
print(name)
print(age)
print(pi)
print(is_student)
```

3. Arithmetic Operations:
```python
# Addition
num1 = 10
num2 = 5
sum = num1 + num2
print("Sum:", sum)

# Subtraction
difference = num1 - num2
print("Difference:", difference)

# Multiplication
product = num1 * num2
print("Product:", product)

# Division
```

```python
quotient = num1 / num2
print("Quotient:", quotient)

# Modulus (Remainder)
remainder = num1 % num2
print("Remainder:", remainder)

# Exponentiation
power = num1 ** num2
print("Power:", power)
```

4. Conditional Statements (if-else):

```python
num = 10

if num > 0:
    print("Positive")
elif num < 0:
    print("Negative")
else:
    print("Zero")
```

5. Loops (for and while):

```python
# For loop example
```

```python
fruits = ["apple", "banana", "cherry"]
for fruit in fruits:
    print(fruit)

# While loop example
i = 0
while i < 5:
    print(i)
    i += 1
```

6. Functions:
```python
def greet(name):
    print("Hello, " + name + "!")

greet("Alice")
```

7. File Handling:
```python
# Reading from a text file
file = open("data.txt", "r")
content = file.read()
print(content)
file.close()
```

```
# Writing to a text file
file = open("data.txt", "w")
file.write("Hello, World!")
file.close()
```

These examples cover a range of fundamental concepts and functionalities in Python programming. Feel free to experiment with them, modify them, and build upon them as you continue to learn and explore Python.

Remember to refer to the relevant sections within the textbook or official Python documentation for a deeper understanding of each topic.

Happy coding!

CONCLUSION

Congratulations on completing this Python textbook! Throughout this journey, you have gained a solid understanding of the fundamentals of Python programming and have acquired the necessary skills to develop various applications.

Python is a versatile and powerful programming language that offers simplicity, readability, and an extensive set of libraries and frameworks. It is widely used in fields such as web development, data science, artificial intelligence, machine learning, and automation.

In this textbook, we started with the basics of Python syntax, data types, and control flow, gradually moving towards more advanced concepts like functions, file handling, and object-oriented programming. We also explored topics such as error handling, modules, and working with external libraries.

By practicing coding exercises and working through hands-on examples, you have not only learned the syntax but also developed problem-solving skills essential for programming. Remember, practice makes perfect, so continue to challenge yourself by solving coding problems and building real-world projects.

As you continue your journey with Python, here are some tips to keep in mind:

1. Stay curious: Python is a dynamic language with a vast ecosystem. There will always be new libraries, frameworks, and techniques to explore. Embrace lifelong learning and continuously seek new knowledge.

2. Read the official documentation: The official Python documentation is an invaluable resource. It provides detailed explanations, examples, and guidelines on using Python and its standard library effectively.

3. Collaborate with others: Join Python communities, forums, or local user groups. Engaging with fellow programmers can help you learn from others' experiences, get feedback on your code, and discover new ways of solving problems.

4. Build real-world projects: Apply your Python skills by developing practical applications and projects. This will not only consolidate your knowledge but also provide you with a portfolio to showcase your abilities to potential employers or clients.

5. Refactor and optimize: As you gain experience, revisit your old code and look for ways to improve it. Refactoring and optimizing code is a crucial skill that can enhance performance, readability, and maintainability.

Remember, coding is a creative process, and there are often multiple solutions to a problem. Find your own coding style and approach that suits you best, while keeping in mind the importance of writing clean and understandable code.

Python is an incredible language with endless possibilities. Whether you choose to pursue web development, data analysis, or machine learning, Python will be a valuable asset in your toolkit.

Lastly, never forget to enjoy the process of learning and coding. Celebrate your achievements, learn from your mistakes, and embrace the challenges that come your way. With persistence, dedication, and the knowledge gained from this textbook, you are equipped to embark on a successful Python programming journey.

Happy coding!

www.ingramcontent.com/pod-product-compliance
Lightning Source LLC
LaVergne TN
LVHW051616050326
832903LV00033B/4522